JANICE VANCLEAVE'S
FIRST-PLACE SCIENCE FAIR PROJECTS™

STEP-BY-STEP SCIENCE EXPERIMENTS IN

BIOLOGY

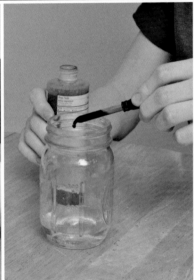

rosen publishing's
rosen central®

NEW YORK

This edition first published in 2013 by:

The Rosen Publishing Group, Inc.
29 East 21st Street
New York, NY 10010

Library of Congress Cataloging-in-Publication Data

VanCleave, Janice Pratt.
Step-by-step science experiments in biology/Janice VanCleave.
    p. cm. — (Janice VanCleave's first-place science fair projects)
Includes bibliographical references and index.
ISBN 978-1-4488-6982-4 (lib. bdg.) —
ISBN 978-1-4488-8463-6 (pbk.) —
ISBN 978-1-4488-8464-3 (6-pack)
1. Biology–Experiments–Juvenile literature. I. Title.
QH316.5.V36 2012
570–dc23

                                                                    2012007943

Manufactured in the United States of America

CPSIA Compliance Information: Batch #S12YA: For further information, contact Rosen Publishing, New York, New York, at
1-800-237-9932.

This edition published by arrangement with and permission of John Wiley & Sons, Inc., Hoboken, New Jersey.

Originally published as *Biology For Every Kid*. Copyright © 1990 by John Wiley & Sons, Inc.

CONTENTS

INTRODUCTION

Biology is the study of the way living organisms behave and interact. The word "biology" originated from two Greek words, *bios* meaning "life" and *logos* meaning "knowledge." This book deals with the study of the knowledge of life, biology. It focuses on three major areas—botany, zoology, and the biology of human beings. A foundation of basic biology facts can assist us in understanding not only ourselves, but our environment—the world around us. Knowing how plants grow can increase food productivity. Understanding cell functions leads to controlling diseases. This book won't help you discover the cure for cancer, but it will offer a key for opening doors leading to future scientific discoveries. Let's take a closer look at the three major areas of study in biology.

Botany is the study of plants, of which there are more than 350,000 types on the earth. People who study plants are called botanists. The word "botany" comes from a Greek word meaning "pasture" or "grass." Ancient Greeks who kept cows needed to know which plants were safe for livestock to eat. Over time, botanists have studied plants in order to learn how they produce oxygen, to discover how to grow enough food for an expanding population, and to help produce medicines and materials used for treating disease.

Zoology is the study of animal life, from simple one-celled organisms to multi-cellular organisms, like mammals.

How organisms live and how their bodies function is of the utmost interest to a zoologist—a person who studies animals. There are a great many kinds of organisms—more than 800,000 kinds of insects, about 9,000 kinds of birds, and snakes, spiders, mammals, and fish. One person cannot know everything about all of these animals. Many scientists specialize and study one type of animal—an ichthyologist studies fish, an entomologist studies insects, and a bacteriologist studies bacteria. In this book, we will study a little about many different animals.

Finally, we have human biology. Studying the human body is a study about yourself. We will barely scratch the surface of all the facts known about the human body, but at the end of this book you will hopefully know more about yourself than before you started. Humans think, reason, feel, and respond with much emotion to the world around us. Scientists have learned a great deal about how the human body functions by studying other organisms and comparing how similar materials respond. You'll get to try a few simple experiments involving human biology in this book.

Biology, as a whole, took a giant step forward less than 400 years ago when Anton van Leeuwenhoek, a Dutch lens grinder, contributed to the perfection and use of the microscope. His curiosity about things led him to making more than 250 different microscopes. Each lens was designed to view a specific object. People visited his home to view through these specially mounted lenses the strange wiggling creatures that Leeuwenhoek called "Wee Beasties." Today, technology has advanced. The electron microscope allows us to view cell parts that were not even dreamed of in Leeuwenhoek's day. But have we discovered everything there is to know about biology? No. The more advanced the tools used, the more questions that arise. We build on the earned knowledge of generations of scientists. Our quest for solutions to mysteries and problems increases with each new discovery. Our knowledge of the universe is very limited, and there are so many questions still to be asked and answered. Even with our vast knowledge of biology there is much to be learned and discovered.

This book takes biology out of the professional laboratory and into your daily life experiences. All of the experiments in this book are basic enough for anyone not familiar with scientific terms to understand. It is designed to present technical biology theories in such a way that someone with little or no scientific training can interpret and understand. The experiments are selected on their ability to be explained very basically and on their lack of complexity. One of the main objectives of this book is to present the fun of biology.

You will be rewarded with successful experiments if you read an experiment carefully, follow each step in order, and do not substitute equipment. There is a standard pattern for each exercise:

1. Purpose: The basic goals for the experiment.
2. Materials: A list of necessary supplies.
3. Procedure: Step-by-step instructions on how to perform the experiment.

4. Results: An explanation stating exactly what is expected to happen. This is an immediate learning tool. If the expected results are achieved, the experimenter has an immediate positive reinforcement. A "foul-up" is also quickly recognized. The need to start over or make corrections will readily be apparent to you.
5. Why?: An explanation of why the results were achieved is described in terms understandable to the reader who may not be familiar with scientific terms.

General Instructions

1. Read: Read each experiment completely before starting.
2. Collect needed supplies: Less frustration and more fun will be experienced if all the necessary materials for the experiments are ready for instant use. You lose your train of thought when you have to stop and search for supplies.
3. Experiment: Do not rush through the experiment. Follow each step very carefully, never skip steps, and do not add your own. Safety is of utmost importance, and by reading any experiment before starting, then following the instructions exactly, you can feel confident that no unexpected results will occur.
4. Observe: If your results are not the same as described in the experiment, carefully reread the instructions, and start over from step one.

And perhaps most important, have fun!

LIMP SPUDS

PURPOSE: To demonstrate two critical conditions that influence osmosis.

MATERIALS:

- table salt
- potato
- measuring cup (250 ml)
- measuring spoon— teaspoon (5 ml)
- two small bowls
- clock

PROCEDURE

1. Mix 3 spoons of salt into 1 cup of water. Pour the salt-water mixture into one of the small bowls.

2. Pour 1 cup of water into the second bowl.

3. Have an adult cut the potato into slices, about one-fourth inch (6 mm) thick.

4. Place half of the potato slices into the bowl of water and the remaining slices into the bowl of salt water.

5. After 15 minutes pick up potato slices from each bowl with your fingers and test their hardness or turgor pressure by trying to bend the slices.
6. What differences do you feel?

RESULTS The potato slices in the water are very stiff and do not bend easily. The slices in the salt water are very limp and bend very easily.

WHY? Two critical factors affecting osmosis are:
1. The amount of water and dissolved material inside the cell.
2. The amount of water and dissolved material outside the cell.

Osmosis is the movement of water across a membrane. Water always moves through a membrane toward the side containing the most dissolved material and the lesser amount of water. In this experiment, the dissolved material will be salt.

Salt and water are only two of the chemicals found inside all potatoes. The potato slices placed in the bowl of water keep the original amount of water in their cells plus more water from the bowl moves into the slices through cell membranes. This extra water makes the slices stiff.

The amount of salt inside each potato slice is less than that mixed with the water in the saltwater mixture. The slices soaked in the salt water feel limp because they have lost some of the original water inside their cells. The water from inside each potato slice moves out of the potato through cell membranes and into the bowl of salt water. The slices are only partially filled and feel limp.

STAND UP

PURPOSE: To demonstrate how the change in turgor pressure causes plant stems to wilt.

MATERIALS:
- 1 drinking glass
- wilted stalk of celery
- blue food coloring

PROCEDURE

1. Ask an adult to cut a slice from the bottom of a wilted celery stalk.

2. Put enough food coloring into a glass half full of water to turn it dark blue.

3. Allow the celery to stand overnight in the blue water.

RESULTS The celery leaves become a blue-green color, and the stalk is firm and crisp.

WHY? A fresh cut across the bottom ensures that the celery cells are not closed off or dried out. Water enters into the water-conducting tubes called xylem. These tubes run the length of the stalk of the celery. Water leaves the xylem tubes and enters the cells up and down the celery stalk. Plants usually stand erect and return to their original position when gently bent. This happens because each plant cell is normally full of water. The water makes each cell firm and all the cells together cause the plant to be rigid. A plant wilts when it is deprived of water and, like half-filled balloons, the cells collapse causing leaves and stems to droop. The pressure of the water inside the plant cell is called turgor pressure.

Living plants can take in water to produce pressure ranging from 60 to 150 pounds per square inch (4 to 10 atmospheres). The pressure becomes so great during rainy seasons that fruits and vegetables can burst. The pressure is enough for growing plants to move rocks and break through concrete.

HARD TO FREEZE

PURPOSE: To determine the effect of dissolved nutrients on the freezing rate of water. How does this affect the freezing rate of plants?

MATERIALS:

- salt
- 2 5-ounce (150 ml) paper cups
- measuring spoon — teaspoon (5 ml)

- refrigerator
- masking tape
- marking pen

PROCEDURE

1. Fill both cups with water, label one salt water and the other water.

13

2. Add 1 spoon of salt to the cup labeled salt water and stir.

3. Place both cups in the freezer.

4. Observe the cups at 2-hour intervals.

RESULTS Salt water never freezes as hard as the pure water.

WHY? Looking at each cup of water you froze, you'll see that salt lowers the freezing point of water. The pure water was able to freeze at a warmer temperature than the salty water.

4 PLANTS BREATHE

PURPOSE: To demonstrate that plants as well as animals exhale carbon dioxide.

MATERIALS:

- distilled water
- 1 quart (1 liter) of purple cabbage indicator
  (see preparation instructions below)
- sprig of Elodea or other water plant (found at pet store)

- 3 pint (500 ml) jars with lids
- straw
- aluminum foil

PROCEDURE

Making the Purple Cabbage Indicator

1. Cut a head of purple cabbage into small pieces. The leaves may be pulled off and torn into small pieces.

2. Place the cabbage pieces in a two-quart bowl.

3. Add enough hot distilled water to fill the bowl.

4. Allow the cabbage to stand until the water cools.

5. Discard the cabbage pieces and save the blue liquid.

Showing that Plants Breathe

1. Rinse the jars with distilled water.
2. Place the Elodea in one of the jars. Fill the jar with purple cabbage indicator.
3. Put the lid on the jar and cover the outside of the jar with aluminum foil.

4. Pour one-half of the remaining cabbage juice into a second jar. Close the lid and cover the outside of the jar with aluminum foil. Position both jars so that they will not be disturbed for 2 days.

5. Pour the remaining cabbage juice into the third jar.

6. Use a straw to exhale into the solution until a color change occurs.

RESULTS The indicator with the plant and the one exhaled into both turn from blue to a reddish color. The third solution is unchanged.

WHY? The indicator contains water and a dye extracted from the purple cabbage. Carbon dioxide from exhaled breath and from the plant combines with the water to form a weak acid called carbonic acid. The cabbage dye turns red when mixed with any acid. Plants produce oxygen by a process called photosynthesis. This requires sunlight. What do they do at night when there is no sun? It is in the dark that they use oxygen and food as do animals, to produce carbon dioxide, water, and energy. This is called respiration.

LEAF COLORS

PURPOSE: To separate and identify color pigments in leaves.

MATERIALS:

- alcohol
- green leaf
- coffee filter
- pencil
- baby food jar
- ruler

PROCEDURE

1. Place the leaf, top side down, on the edge of the coffee filter.

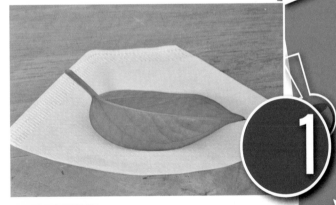

2. Rub the pencil lead back and forth ten times over the leaf about one half inch (13 mm) from the edge of the paper.

19

3. Rotate the leaf and repeat step 2. Continue moving and marking on the leaf until a single dark green spot forms on the filter paper.

4. Cut a one-half inch (13 mm) strip to the center of the filter.

5. Bend the strip down to form a tab.

6. Place the filter on top of the jar with the bent tab inside the jar.

7. Lift the filter and slowly pour alcohol into the jar to a depth that allows the bottom of the paper tab to barely touch the liquid. Important: Be sure the alcohol level is below the green dot on the paper.

8. Allow the paper to sit undisturbed for 30 minutes.

RESULTS The alcohol starts to move up the paper tab, and the green dot dissolves in it. As the green alcohol solution climbs up the paper, the green color stops and a yellow streak forms.

WHY? Plants contain several color pigments that are necessary in the food production reaction called photosynthesis. The green pigment is the most abundant, causing most plant leaves to appear green in color. Another pigment is present, but in smaller quantities. It is called carotenoid and ranges in color from red to yellow. Carotenoid is responsible for the color of fruits and flowers. The beautiful colors of fall leaves are due to the fact that chlorophyll stops being formed first, leaving carotenoid to display its colors.

Living things are composed of many different chemicals. You have just used the process called paper chromatography to separate and observe two of the many. Chromatography means "to write with color." The chemicals dissolve in the alcohol and move up the paper. The heavier material settles out first, allowing separation of the lighter substances from the heavier ones.

GROW A BEAN

PURPOSE: To determine if it matters how seeds are planted.

MATERIALS:

- 4 pinto pole beans
- paper towels
- masking tape
- one drinking glass
- marking pen

PROCEDURE

1. Fold a paper towel, and line the inside of the glass with it.

1

2. Wad paper towels and stuff them into the glass to hold the paper lining tightly against the glass.

3. Place a strip of tape around the outside of the glass about halfway up the glass.

4. On four sides of the glass, mark the tape with an arrow to indicate the directions of up, down, left, and right.

5. Place one bean to the right of each directional arrow. Make sure the bean's hilum is pointing in the direction indicated by the arrow.

6. Moisten the paper in the glass with water. You do not want the paper to be dripping wet—only moist.

7. Keep the paper moist and observe for 7 days.

RESULTS No matter which direction the bean is planted, the roots grow down and the stems upward. It takes about 7 days for measurable results.

WHY? Plants contain auxin, a chemical that changes the speed of plant growth. Gravity causes the auxin to collect in the lower part of the plant structure. Stem cells grow faster on the side where there is more auxin, causing the stem to bend upward. Root cells grow faster on the side where there is a smaller amount of auxin, causing this section to bend downward. The end result is that auxin causes stems to grow up and roots to grow down.

FLOWER MAZE

PURPOSE: To observe a plant winding its way toward light.

MATERIALS:

- shoebox with a lid
- paper cup
- three pinto beans
- potting soil
- cardboard
- scissors
- tape

PROCEDURE

1. Fill the cup with potting soil.

2. Plant the beans in the soil.

3. Moisten the soil and allow the beans to sprout (about 5 to 7 days).

25

4. Cut two cardboard pieces to fit inside the shoebox.
5. Secure the cardboard with tape to form a maze.
6. Cut a hole in the lid.

7. Place the bean plant inside the shoebox at one end.

8. Secure the box lid with the hole on the opposite end from the plant.
9. Open the lid daily to observe the plant's growth.
10. Water the soil when needed.

11. Continue to observe until the plant grows out the hole in the lid.

RESULTS The plant winds around the obstacles and out the hole in the lid.

WHY? The plant is growing toward the light. This movement toward light is called phototropism. A buildup of auxin, a plant growth chemical, occurs on the dark side of the stem. Auxin causes cells to grow longer on the dark side. This forces the stem to bend toward light. After a few weeks, your plant will find its way to the light.

ALGAE GROWTH

PURPOSE: To grow algae.

MATERIALS:

- clear, glass jar
- pond water

(collect from a lake, pond, or an aquarium that needs cleaning)

- pond plant

(may be found at a pet store or lake)

PROCEDURE

1. Add the water to the jar.

2. Place the plant in the water.

3. Place the jar near a window that receives direct sunlight.

4. Examine the jar after 7 days and then after 14 days.

RESULTS The color of the water becomes increasingly green.

WHY? There are 30,000 different kinds of algae. Many are green due to the abundance of a green pigment called chlorophyll. Algae makes its own food, as do other plants, by a process called photosynthesis. The necessary requirements for this reaction are carbon dioxide, water, light, and chlorophyll. The algae grows in its sunny, watery environment producing more and more cells that contain the green chlorophyll. As the number of these cells increases, the water becomes greener in color.

Some algae are brown and some are red. It is the abundance of red algae that gives the water in the Red Sea its reddish color.

WATERLOGGED

PURPOSE: To determine why plants grow in sphagnum (peat moss).

MATERIALS:

- sphagnum moss (obtain from a garden supply store)
- soil (collect from a garden, under a tree, or a vacant lot)
- 2 quart (liter) jars
- measuring spoon— tablespoon (15 ml)
- measuring cup (250 ml)

PROCEDURE

1. Pour 1 cup of soil into a jar, and 1 cup of sphagnum moss into the remaining jar.

2. Add 1 spoon of water to the moss and observe any results.

3. Continue to add water to the moss 1 spoon at a time until it will no longer soak up the water. Record the amount of water added.

4. Repeat the process by adding water 1 spoon at a time to the jar containing the soil.

5. Record the amount of water that must be added before the soil no longer is able to soak it up.

6. What would be the advantage of using sphagnum to grow plants in?

RESULTS The sphagnum moss is able to soak up much more water than the soil.

WHY? Sphagnum moss is commonly called peat moss and is used in growing plants. The moss acts like a dry sponge with cavities that the water can move into. Gardeners often mix the moss with soil or spread it around plants because the moss holds so much water. It also is used in potting plants that must be shipped to assure that they stay moist.

At one time, physicians used this moss to cover wounds because it absorbed liquids so well. It was observed that wounds bound with the moss became infected less often than those covered with other dressings.

MINI-ORGANISMS

PURPOSE: To test the effect of preservatives on bacterial growth.

MATERIALS:

- table salt
- white vinegar
- 3 small clear glasses
- 1 chicken bouillon cube
- 1 measuring cup (250 ml)
- 1 measuring spoon— teaspoon (5 ml)
- masking tape
- marking pen

PROCEDURE

1. Dissolve the bouillon cube in one cup (250 ml) of hot water from the faucet.

2. Equally divide the solution among the three glasses.

3. Add 1 spoon of salt to the first glass and label the glass "salt" as in the diagram; make the label with the masking tape.

4. Add 1 spoon of vinegar to the second glass and label it "vinegar."

5. The last glass is to be labeled "control" because it will not contain a preservative.

6. Place the three glasses in a warm place for 2 days. Which glass is cloudier when the time is up?

RESULTS The solution containing vinegar should be clearer than the others. The control should be the most cloudy. The salt solution should be somewhat cloudy.

WHY? The cloudiness is due to the presence of large quantities of bacteria. The glasses containing preservatives are clearer than the control because the preservatives inhibit, or slow down, the growth of bacteria. Vinegar seems to have inhibited the bacterial growth the best.

FUZZ BALLS

PURPOSE: To determine the best environment for penicillium growth.

MATERIALS:

- cotton balls
- 2 oranges
- 2 lemons
- 2 bread sacks
- bowl

PROCEDURE

1. Rub the fruit on the floor.

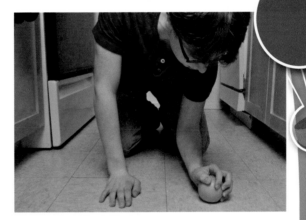

2. Place the fruit in a bowl exposed to the air for one day.

3. Place in each bread sack an orange, a lemon, and a cotton ball wet with water.

4. Secure the ends of the sacks.

5. Place one sack in the refrigerator and the other in a warm, dark place.

6. Leave the sacks closed for two weeks.

7. Observe the fruit through the sacks daily.

RESULTS The fruit in the refrigerator looks the same or possibly a bit dryer, but the other fruit has turned into blue-green fuzzy balls.

WHY? The green powdery growth on the outside of the fruit is penicillium. Under a microscope this mold looks like a small brush, thus it was named from the Latin word *penicillus* meaning a paintbrush. Because brushes were used to write with at one time, our modern writing tool, the pencil, is named after the Latin word for paintbrush. Molds can grow in hot places, but they grow faster and in more abundance in moist warm places. This is why foods become moldier in the summertime. Placing bread in a breadbox or on top of a refrigerator causes them to mold more quickly. Cooling foods slows down the growth of mold and freezing keeps foods fresh for much longer periods of time.

DECOMPOSERS

PURPOSE: To observe the effects of yeast on food decomposition.

MATERIALS:

- banana
- 2 plastic sandwich bags
- dry yeast
- teaspoon (5 ml)
- marker

PROCEDURE

1. Ask an adult to cut 2 slices from the banana.

2. Place a slice of banana inside each plastic bag.

3. Sprinkle one-half of a spoon of yeast on one of the banana slices.

4. Close both bags.

5. Mark the bag containing the yeast with a Y.

6. Check each bag for one week. Which banana slice shows the most and fastest decomposition?

RESULTS The banana covered with yeast shows the most and fastest decomposition.

WHY? Yeast is one of 100,000 different kinds of organisms that make up the fungi group. They all are lacking chlorophyll and must depend on other organisms for food. The yeast feeds on the banana causing it to break into smaller parts. This breakdown is referred to as decay. Decomposers are an important part of our world because there is much dead material that must be broken into smaller parts and reused by plants and animals. The fertilizer used on plants and gardens has many decomposers working in it to make the material usable by the plants.

EQUAL PRESSURE

PURPOSE: To demonstrate how fish cells respond to fresh and salty water.

MATERIALS:

- salt
- measuring spoon— teaspoon (5 ml)
- 2 shallow bowls
- 1 small cucumber
- masking tape
- marker

PROCEDURE

1. Fill both bowls one-half full with water.

2. Stir 1 spoon of salt into one of the bowls, label this bowl "salt" using the tape to make the label.

43

3. Have an adult cut the cucumber into thin circular slices.

4. Place 3 slices of cucumber into each bowl.

5. Wait 30 minutes.

6. Remove the slices and test their flexibility by carefully using your fingers to bend them back and forth.

7. Now switch the slices, placing the ones that were previously in the salt water into the pure water, and the pure water slices go into the salty water.

8. Wait 30 minutes and again test the flexibility.

RESULTS The cucumber slices are limp after soaking in the salt water and firmer in the pure water.

WHY? Water moves into and out of living cells through the cell membrane. This movement is called osmosis. The water moves across the membrane toward where there are more dissolved materials in the water. Water moves out of the cells into the surrounding salty water because there are more salt particles in the water in the bowl than there is inside the cell. Removal of water is called dehydration. Fish in salt water tend to dehydrate and they compensate for this water loss from their cells by drinking large amounts of seawater. They excrete salt from their gills, and their kidneys remove very little water from the body. Freshwater fish, however, would bloat because the opposite happens to them. Water is absorbed into their cells. The surrounding medium is less salty. Therefore, they excrete large amounts of water through their kidneys. Both types of fish have to compensate for the loss and gain of water by their cells due to their environment.

EXPERIMENT 14 EARTHWORM FARM

PURPOSE: To produce an environment suitable for earthworms.

MATERIALS:

- 1 quart (liter) jar
- 2 cups (500 ml) of soil
- 1 cup (250 ml) humus
  (partially decayed leaves and roots)

- earthworms (from a bait shop or dig your own)
- apple peels
- dark construction paper
- rubberband

PROCEDURE

1. Pour the soil into the jar.
2. Moisten the soil with the water.

3. Sprinkle the humus over the soil.

4. Put the worms into the jar.

5. Add the apple peels.

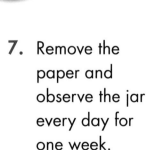

6. Wrap the paper around the jar and secure with a rubber-band. Place the jar in a cool place.

7. Remove the paper and observe the jar every day for one week.

RESULTS The worms start wiggling and burrow into the soil. Tunnels are seen in the soil after a few days. The apple peelings disappear and casts appear on the surface of the soil.

WHY? Earthworms are very beneficial because they loosen and enrich the soil. On the average, there are 50,000 worms per acre (4,047 square meters) of soil and they eat about 18 wagonloads of soil every year. They do not have a jaw or teeth, but a muscle draws soil particles into their mouth. The worm extracts food from the soil and the remaining part of the soil passes through the worm's body unchanged. Casts containing the undigested soil are deposited on the surface of the soil.

It is important to keep the soil moist because it is through their moist skin that earthworms absorb the oxygen found in the air spaces throughout the soil.

GROUND TEMPERATURE

PURPOSE: To determine why desert animals spend their day underground.

MATERIALS:
- 2 outdoor thermometers
- trowel
- white towel

PROCEDURE

1. Dig a hole 4 inches (10 cm) deep and large enough to insert one thermometer.

2. Cover the hole containing the thermometer with the towel.

49

3. Lay the second thermometer on top of the ground.

4. Wait 5 minutes, then read the temperature on each thermometer. Be sure to read the underground thermometer as soon as it is removed from the ground.

RESULTS The temperature in the hole is lower than that on top of the ground.

WHY? The sun's rays heat the air and all materials that they touch including the liquid in the thermometer. The soil on top of the ground gets much hotter because of the direct sun's rays. The soil in the hole stays cooler because no direct heat is applied. Desert animals dig holes into the ground and stay there during the heat of the day to stay cool.

16 OILY FEATHERS

PURPOSE: To demonstrate the effect that polluting detergents can have on birds.

MATERIALS:

- 1 quart (1 liter) clear glass bowl
- measuring cup (250 ml)
- liquid oil
- powdered washing detergent
- teaspoon (5 ml)

PROCEDURE

1. Pour 1 cup of water into the bowl.

2. Add 1 spoon of liquid oil.

3. Observe the surface of the water.

4. Sprinkle 2 spoons of powdered detergent over the surface of the liquid.

5. Gently stir the water to mix, but try not to produce bubbles.

6. Again observe the surface of the water.

RESULTS The oil spread out in large circles on the surface of the water before the addition of the detergent. When the detergent was added, some of the oil sank and the rest broke up into tiny bubbles that covered the water's surface.

WHY? Water is heavier and does not mix with oil, thus the oil was able to float on the water's surface. Detergent molecules stick to water on one side and the detergent's opposite side sticks to the oil. The large circles of oil no longer exist because there are molecules of the detergent, which allows the oil and water to mix. Detergents can cause a swimming bird to sink and drown. Birds stay afloat because of the oil on their feathers. The birds are waterproof. If the birds become soaked in water containing a high concentration of detergent, the natural oil in the birds' feathers would break up into tiny droplets and allow water to penetrate the feathers. The bird would lose its waterproofing and the extra water on the feathers would increase the bird's weight and it would sink.

IN BUT NOT OUT

PURPOSE: To observe the movement of particles through a membrane.

MATERIALS:

- 1 plastic sandwich bag
- 1 twist tie
- tincture of iodine
- cornstarch
- 2 measuring cups (500 ml)
- eye dropper
- measuring spoon—
  tablespoon (15 ml)

PROCEDURE

1. Fill a cup one-half full with water, and add 20 drops of iodine.

2. Fill a second cup with water and stir in one spoon of cornstarch.

3. Pour one-half of the starch and water mixture into the plastic bag.

4. Use the twist tie to secure the top of the bag.

5. Rinse off any starch and water mixture that might have dropped onto the outside of the bag.

6. Place the bag in the cup of water and iodine.

7. Observe any changes immediately and then again after 30 minutes.

8. While waiting for changes to occur inside the bag add 5 drops of iodine to the remaining starch and water mixture in the cup.

RESULTS The iodine turns the starch and water mixture in the cup black. The iodine does not turn the water in the bowl black, but after a while the contents of the plastic bag turn black.

WHY? Iodine is used to test for the presence of starch since a purple-black color forms when the two materials are mixed. The water in the bowl never turned black, indicating the absence of starch in the water. The iodine particles are small enough to move through the tiny holes in the plastic bag, but the starch molecules are too large to pass through. The inside of the bag turned black because the iodine passed through the membrane and mixed with the starch inside. The water outside contains iodine, but the starch was unable to move out of the bag, thus no color change. The plastic bag represents a cell membrane with cell parts inside. Materials are able to move into and out of the cell through this membrane. This movement of materials through a membrane from a concentrated area to a less concentrated area is called diffusion.

NAKED EGG

PURPOSE: To demonstrate the semi-permeability of a cell membrane.

MATERIALS:

- 1 raw egg in its shell
- 1 jar with a lid (the egg must fit inside the jar)
- clear vinegar
- flexible measuring tape

PROCEDURE

1. Measure and record the circumference around the center of the egg.
2. Record the appearance of the egg.

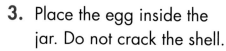

3. Place the egg inside the jar. Do not crack the shell.

4. Cover the egg with vinegar.

5. Close the lid.

6. Observe immediately and then periodically for the next 72 hours.

7. Remove the egg after 72 hours and measure its circumference.

8. Compare the appearance of the egg before and after being in the vinegar.

9. How has the egg changed in appearance and size?

RESULTS The egg has a hard shell on the outside and the circumference will vary. Bubbles start forming on the surface of the egg's shell immediately and increase in number with time. After 72 hours, the shell will be gone and portions of it may be seen floating on the surface of the vinegar. The egg remains intact because of the thin see-through membrane. The size of the egg has increased.

WHY? The shell of the egg is made of calcium carbonate, commonly called limestone. When vinegar chemically reacts with the limestone, one of the products is carbon dioxide gas, those bubbles seen on the egg. The membrane around the egg does not dissolve in vinegar, but becomes more rubbery. The increased size is due to osmosis, the movement of water through a cell membrane. The water in the vinegar moves through the thin membrane into the egg because the water inside the egg has more materials dissolved in it than does the vinegar. Water will always move through a membrane in the direction where there are more dissolved materials. The contents of the egg stayed inside the membrane because these molecules were too large to pass through the tiny holes. This selectiveness of materials moving through the membrane is called semi-permeability.

HAVE AN ONION

PURPOSE: To determine your sensitivity to taste.

MATERIALS:
- toothpicks
- blindfold
- spring-type clothespin
- apple
- onion

PROCEDURE

1. Have an adult peel and cut the apple and onion into small bite-size pieces of equal size.

2. Ask a helper to assist you with the experiment. Without seeing or smelling, the person will decide on the identity of the food by taste only.

3. Blindfold the helper and place the clothespin on his or her nose. An old clothespin with a weak spring is best so that it will not pinch too tightly.

4. Use a toothpick to place a piece of apple in the helper's mouth and give instructions to chew it and identify what the food is. It is important that the helper has not seen the food samples before the experiment starts.

5. After making an identification, have your helper remove the nose clip and compare the taste when odor is included.

6. Replace the clip and blindfold, then use a toothpick to place the onion piece in your helper's mouth.

7. Ask for an identification.

8. Remove the clip and again ask for an identification.

RESULTS Without smelling, the apple and onion have a similar taste. The texture of the food will give clues, but the taste is the same.

WHY? The tongue has nerve endings that allow one to taste things that are sweet, sour, salty, or bitter. Most of the taste sensations experienced are due to smell. Make a note of how tasteless food seems the next time you have a cold and cannot breathe properly.

NEGATIVE AFTERIMAGE

PURPOSE: To experience the effect of tiring the rods and cones in the eye.

MATERIALS:

- scissors
- glue
- notebook paper
- green, black, and yellow construction paper

PROCEDURE

1. Use construction paper to make the American flag, but instead of it being red, white, and blue it will be green, black, and yellow.
2. Alternate green and black strips of paper for the stripes.
3. The stars are to be black on a yellow background.

4. Glue all the colored pieces to a sheet of notebook paper.

4

5. After the flag has been constructed, stare at the center of the flag for one full minute. Make an effort not to move your eyes around and blink as few times as possible.

6. After the minute of staring, look at a white wall or piece of paper. Blink several times.

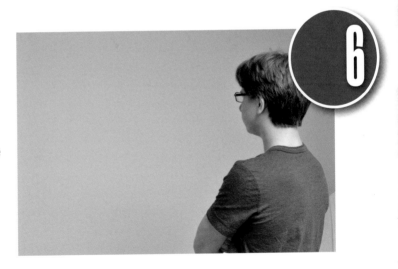

RESULTS The American flag with its true colors of red, white, and blue seem to appear on the white surface.

WHY? On the retina of the eye are light sensitive receivers called cones. They are sensitive to colors of red, blue, and green. You see colors because light enters your eye and stimulates the cones. Light from colors other than red, blue, or green, such as yellow, stimulates two or all three of the cones. Prolonged stimulation, such as staring at the colored flag, tires or desensitizes the cones hit by light coming from the different colors. Then when you look at the white paper, light reflecting from the paper shines on your retina and equally stimulates all the cones. The tired cones do not respond well, but the rested cones send strong messages. Normally the afterimage of green will appear as red, the afterimage of black will appear as white, and the afterimage of yellow will appear as blue. This results in the afterimage of the flag appearing to be red, white, and blue.

SMALL INTESTINE

PURPOSE: To demonstrate the movement of soluble materials through the lining of the small intestine.

MATERIALS:

- sugar
- cornstarch
- tincture of iodine
  (purchase at a pharmacy)
- funnel
- round coffee filters
  (large enough to fit inside the funnel)

- 1 glass jar
- 1 small drinking glass
- 1 measuring cup (250 ml)
- tablespoon (15 ml)
- eye dropper

PROCEDURE

1. Line the funnel with 5 coffee filters.

2. Place the stem of the funnel in the jar.

3. Mix 1 spoon of cornstarch and 1 spoon of sugar with 1 cup of water.

4. Pour three-fourths of the starch and water solution into the funnel. Be sure that the liquid does not spill over the top edge of the funnel into the jar.

5. Pour a few drops of the liquid that has passed through the filter paper into a small drinking glass. Taste this colorless liquid. *Note:* Never taste anything in a laboratory setting unless you are sure that it that it contains no harmful chemicals. This experiment is safe since the liquid only contains water, sugar, and cornstarch.

6. Add 3 drops of tincture of iodine to the remaining liquid that passed through the filter paper. DO NOT taste. Note the color produced.

7. Add 3 drops of tincture of iodine to the remaining starch, sugar, and water solution in the cup. Note the color.

RESULTS The sugar, starch, and water solution turns a purple-black color when the tincture of iodine is added. The liquid that passed through the filter paper tastes sweet and turns a pale amber color with no shades of purple when the iodine is added.

WHY? Iodine is used to test for the presence of starch. A purple color results when iodine and starch combine. The lack of a purple color in the liquid that passed through the filter paper indicates that starch did not pass through the paper. The lining of the small intestine, like the filter paper, allows small molecules to pass through, but the large starch molecules cannot get through the small holes in the paper or the intestine lining. The sugar, sucrose, used in this experiment is small enough to pass through the filter paper and it is a much larger molecule than glucose, the sugar that passes through the intestine lining.

22 SIZE CHANGE

PURPOSE: To determine if some digestion occurs in the mouth.

MATERIALS:

- saltine cracker
- tincture of iodine
  (purchase at a pharmacy)
- eye dropper
- 2 small jars
- tablespoon (15 ml)

PROCEDURE

1. Break the cracker in two.

2. Crumble one half of the cracker into a clean jar.

3. Add 2 spoons of water to the jar containing the cracker and stir well.

4. Add 3 drops of tincture of iodine and stir. Observe the color.

5. Chew the remaining piece of cracker for 1 minute or until it is a liquid mush. You want as much saliva as possible to combine with the cracker.

6. Spit the cracker-saliva mixture into an empty, clean jar. Add 2 spoons of water and stir.

71

7. Add 3 drops of tincture of iodine and stir. Observe the color.

8. Compare the color of the liquids in both jars. What causes the difference?

RESULTS Tincture of iodine added to the cracker and water produces a purple to black color. The chewed cracker produces a much paler color when the iodine is added.

WHY? Iodine is used to test for the presence of starch. Any starchy substance will turn purple when touched by iodine. Chewing the cracker mixes it with saliva. Chemicals called enzymes in saliva change starch molecules into a sugar called glucose. Iodine has no effect on glucose thus the color of the chewed cracker plus iodine is a pale purple because most of the starch has been changed to glucose. This change of starch to glucose is part of the digestive process and this experiment demonstrates that digestion does occur in the mouth.

GLOSSARY

auxin A chemical that changes the speed of plant growth.

carotenoid Plant pigment used in photosynthesis; its color ranges from red to yellow.

casts Undigested soil deposited by earthworms.

cell membrane A thin skin-like structure around the outside of cells.

chromatography The word means to write with color. It is a method of separating mixtures.

cones Light sensitive receivers on the retina; allows one to see color.

dehydration Movement of water out of a cell.

diffusion Spontaneous movement of molecules from one place to another resulting in a uniform mixture.

indicator Solution used to test for the presence of an acid or base.

mold A form of fungus.

osmosis The movement of water from an area with a great amount of water to an area with a lesser amount of water.

penicillium Greenish mold found on food; used to make medicine. Word "penicillus" means paintbrush. The name penicillium was given to the mold because it looks like a brush.

photosynthesis Food-making reaction in plants. It uses carbon dioxide, water, and sunlight to produce oxygen and sugar.

phototropism Plant growth in response to light.

respiration A reaction in plants and animals that uses oxygen and sugar to produce carbon dioxide, water, and energy.

retina Back layer of the eyeball where images are focused by the lens.

semi-permeable membrane A material that allows different sized materials to pass through it.

turgor pressure Pressure of water inside cells.

xylem Tiny tubes in the stalk of a plant stem; transports water and food to the plant cells.

American Association for the Advancement of Science
1200 New York Avenue NW
Washington, DC 20005
(202) 326-6400
Web site: http://www.aaas.org
An international nonprofit organization dedicated to advancing
science around the world by serving as an educator,
leader, spokesperson, and professional association.

American Museum of Natural History
Central Park West at 79th Street
New York, NY 10024-5192
(212) 769-5100
Web site: http://www.amnh.org
Museum showcasing hundreds of animal species and fossils
from the history of life on Earth.

Columbus Zoo
4850 West Powell Road
Powell, OH 43065
(800) MONKEYS
Web site: http://www.columbuszoo.org
One of the top-rated zoos in the United States, with over
7,000 animals.

Michigan State University
Department of Zoology
203 Natural Sciences Building

East Lansing, MI 48824-1115
(517) 355-4640
Web site: http://www.zoology.msu.edu
One of the top zoology departments in the United States for
    students seeking a career in zoology.

San Diego Zoo
2920 Zoo Drive
San Diego, CA 92101
(619) 231-1515
Web site: http://www.sandiegozoo.org
One of the top-rated zoos in the United States, including a
    giant panda exhibit—one of four in the world.

Sternberg Museum of Natural History
3000 Sternberg Drive
Hays, KS 67601
(877) 332-1165
Web site: http://sternberg.fhsu.edu
A museum that advances an appreciation and understanding
    of Earth's natural history and the evolutionary forces that
    impact it.

University of Hawaii at Manoa
Department of Zoology
2540 Campus Road, Dean Hall Room 2
Honolulu, HI 96822

(808) 956-8617
Web site: http://www.hawaii.edu/zoology
One of the top zoology departments in the United States for students seeking a career in zoology.

WEB SITES

Due to the changing nature of Internet links, Rosen Publishing has developed an online list of Web sites related to the subject of this book. This site is updated regularly. Please use this link to access the list:

http://www.rosenlinks.com/scif/bio

FOR FURTHER READING

Bardhan-Quallen, Sudipta. *Kitchen Science Experiments: How Does Your Mold Garden Grow?* New York, NY: Sterling, 2010.

Benbow, Ann, and Colin Mably. *Awesome Animal Science Projects*. Berkeley Heights, NJ: Enslow, 2009.

Calhoun, Yael. *Plant and Animal Science Fair Projects*. Berkeley Heights, NJ: Enslow, 2010.

DK Publishing. *First Nature Encyclopedia*. New York, NY: DK, 2006.

Gardner, Robert. *Easy Genius Science Projects with the Human Body: Great Experiments and Ideas*. Berkeley Heights, NJ: Enslow, 2008.

Gray, Susan H. *Super Cool Science Experiments: Seeds*. North Mankato, MN: Cherry Lake, 2009.

Kurzwell, Allen, and Max Kurzwell. *Potato Chip Science: 29 Incredible Experiments*. New York, NY: Workman, 2010.

Leslie, Clare Walker. *The Nature Connection: An Outdoor Workbook for Kids, Families, and Classrooms*. North Adams, MA: Storey, 2010.

Walker, Pam, and Elaine Wood. *Ecosystem Science Fair Projects*. Berkeley Heights, NJ: Enslow, 2010.

Young, Karen Romano. *Science Fair Winners: Experiments to Do on Your Family*. Des Moines, IA: National Geographic, 2010.

INDEX

ABOUT THE AUTHOR

Janice VanCleave is a former award-winning science teacher who now spends her time writing and giving hands-on science workshops. She is the author of more than forty children's science books.

Designer: Nicole Russo; Editor: Bethany Bryan

All photos by Cindy Reiman, assisted by Karen Huang.